Francis Gary
and
Walter Pfenninger

To Chris
Best wishes
Fun Gary Powers

Enemy Territory

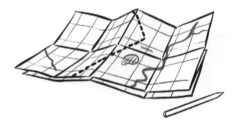

Dedicated to all Cold War veterans

Special thanks to Dr. Douglas E. Campbell and Jonathan B. Teperson, Esq. for their assistance with editing and proofreading.

As well as my wife, son, and sister for their continued love and support.

www.coldwar.org

German Version:
Walter Pfenninger
Feindgebiet

English Version:
Francis Gary Powers, Jr. and Walter Pfenninger
Enemy Territory

Coloring and handwritten letter texts: Monika Pfenninger

Published by GaryPowers.com

Printed by Lulu Press Inc.

ISBN 978-0-578-26914-6

After World War II (1939-1945), which ended soon after the dropping of the atomic bombs on Hiroshima and Nagasaki, the United States and other western Allies accused the Soviet Union of aggressively spreading communism. The world divided into two blocs, East and West. The result was a war that was not fought with traditional weaponry, but clandestinely, in the shadows, called the "Cold War." Two superpowers, the United States and the Soviet Union, engaged in a seemingly endless struggle for technological supremacy, accumulated huge arsenals of atomic weapons, and spied on each other.

The following story, based on true events, is set in this period.

GERMAN DEMOCRATIC REPUBLIC (GDR), SATURDAY, FEBRUARY 10, 1962

POTSDAM

POTSDAM 7:45 A.M.

CLACK

Hello Mr. Powers.

My name Shishkin.

It's going to work like this. We go on the bridge at 8:20 a.m. Another group of Americans will do the same from the other side.

Part of the group will meet in the middle of the bridge. If everything is satisfactory you will walk to the white line.

If something goes wrong, we turn back. Do you understand?

Yes.

I will not turn back even if it means a bullet.

An American is coming across the border.

Hey, good to see you again!

You know who I am, don't you?

You're Bill.

No, I'm Murphy, ...

... Bill was our boss. You got the names mixed up.

What was your high school football coach's name?*

Even though he doesn't remember,...

* Question Powers entered on a form when he joined the United States Air Force, and which was intended to serve as confirmation of identification.

The story of the
American CIA U-2 pilot
Francis Gary Powers.

Risk is called for.

Francis Gary Powers, born on 17 August 1929 in Burdine, Kentucky, is the second of six children of Oliver and Ida Powers. The other five are girls. His father works as a coal miner. He wants Francis to become a doctor. When he is about twelve years old Francis and his father take a trip to West Virginia. At a small airfield in Princeton, Francis's father buys him a flight in a two-seater airplane. The female pilot is so impressed by his enthusiasm that they stay up there twice as long. Francis knows from that moment on: "My heart is up there."

The father is injured in a mining accident. The family buys a small farm and a cobbler's shoe shop in Pound, Virginia. Francis is the first of his family to attend College. Upon graduating Milligan College in 1950, he is not interested in going to medical school.

Instead, he enlists in the United States Air Force. In 1950 Powers was commissioned as a Second Lieutenant and is stationed at Turner Air Force Base near Albany, Georgia. There he marries eighteen-year-old Barbara Gay Moore, whose mother works at the Air Force base.

To get a better salary, Francis seeks a job with a civilian airline at the end of 1955. But he learns that at twenty-six and a half, he is too old for the job.

TURNER AIR FORCE BASE, ALBANY, GEORGIA, JANUARY 1956

Hey Powers, you on the list too.

What list?

It's about a pilot job. We report tomorrow.

THE NEXT MORNING

Meeting place: Radium Springs Inn. Room No. 1. You identify yourselves and ask for Mr. Collins.

Powers, you are up at 7 p.m.

JUST BEFORE 7 P.M.

... sleep on it. One more thing, you will be in Europe for 18 months without family.

I've only been married nine months!

Discuss it with your wife, but don't tell anyone else.

LATER As adventurous as the job may be, I don't want to jeopardize our happiness.

But we could use the the money. And 18 months is not forever.

Do you really think so, Barbara?

THE NEXT DAY We're with the CIA. Are you ready to sign a contract with us?

Does the thought of flying a plane higher than any human being has ever flown interest you?

In the training phase you earn $1,500 per month. Later in Europe it will be $2,500*!

You ask yourself what kind of job justifies such a high salary.

* Equivelent to $16,000 to $26,000 in 2022

6

7

The U-2

Using a cover story as a civilian employee of the United States Air Force, Powers travels under the name Palmer in January 1956 to Washington DC.

11

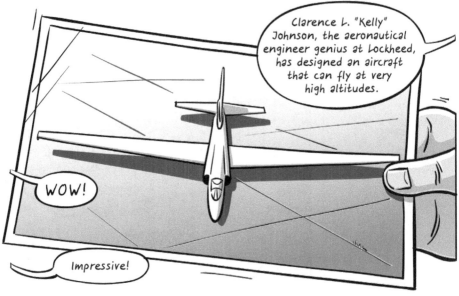

After a lie detector test, that leaves nothing to the imagination, and several meetings in various hotels, the pilots are sent to the Lovelace Clinic in Albuquerque, New Mexico to undergo physical tests.
Some of the tests are later also used on American astronauts.

Did you get through the claustrophobia test, Buster?

Yeah, it was tough. I'll be glad when all the tests are finally over and we can fly again.

I feel the same way. After all, we are pilots.

BACK IN ALBANY

I've missed you.

I missed you too.

In a few weeks I will be gone again for a long time.

13

Watertown Strip is located in a desert in southern Nevada at a salt lake. A place of absolute isolation - far away from everything. Normally, you can only get there by plane. Here, the pilots are familiarized with the U-2s and their peculiarities.

In order to save as much weight as possible, the support wheels on the wings, called Pogos, drop off after takeoff.

The U-2 rapidly gains altitude and is out of sight within a few minutes.
Almost daily new altitude records are being broken.

This rate of climb is fantastic!

SUDDENLY

A Flameout?!

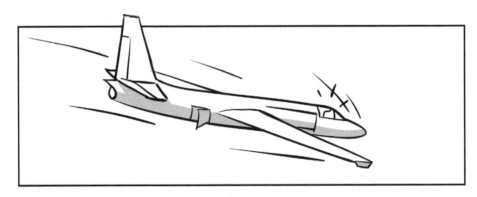

* Francis is called Frank by his friends

The pilots are officially employees of the National Advisory Committee for Aeronautics (NACA), a government organization, which is involved in basic aviation research. In addition, they also learn how to use sensitive cameras and sensors, whose optics are about six times sharper than the human eye.
NACA later became the National Aeronautics and Space Administration (NASA).

At a secret CIA farm on the East Coast, the pilots are also taught survival strategies in the event of going down over enemy territory.

Based on the knowledge that such distinctive aircraft will not go undetected they will be officially deployed in a weather observation program based in Europe. The planes are dismantled and flown to Europe. The pilots are given a two-week vacation.

POUND, VIRGINIA, AUGUST 1956

You enjoy the collection of weather data?

I sure do Dad.

And you don't mind being away from Barbara for so long?

Well, I'm sure it will be a hard time, but that's what we've decided.

AT THE AIRPORT

I will miss you.

I'll miss you too, Frank.

Maybe I can get some time off for Christmas.

And I will write you as often as possible.

Me too.

I'll call again briefly to the house.

Hi, daddy, I just wanted to say goodbye.

I realize now what you're doing, Francis.

What do you mean by that? Have I told you what I'm doing?

No, I figured it out. You work for the FBI!

Goodbye daddy, gotta go.

Powers is flying with the Second Weather Observation Squadron Detachment 10-10 to Europe. Destination: Incirlik Air Base near Adana, Turkey.

Europe

Incirlik Air Base is located 8 miles* from the center of Adana. The base is mainly used for refueling American aircraft. For the time being, the pilots are busy making the aircraft ready to fly again.

WEEKS LATER

Hey Bob, are you coming to Adana for dinner?

Buster is coming too.

Sure!

Finally, a good meal.

Yes, the food on the base leaves a lot to be desired.

END OF OCTOBER 1956

each other ...
I miss you!
All love
Frank

NOVEMBER 4, 1956

It's your turn Powers.

When, Colonel?

If the weather stays good, in a couple of days.

THE NIGHT BEFORE THE FLIGHT

The only difference from other flights is that it takes longer and is over the Soviet Union.

LATER

Crap, I can't sleep!!

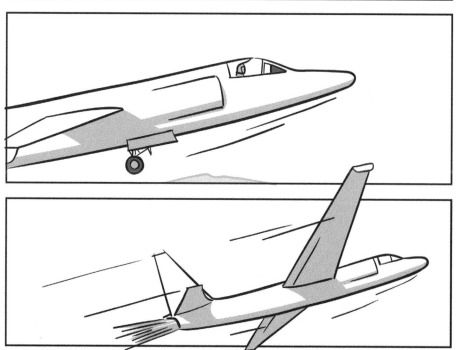

In close proximity to the Soviet border, pilots use a code in radio communication. The pilot indicates the intention to continue the flight by clicking the radio button twice. The base acknowledges with a single click. Three clicks: immediate return to base.

* The U-2 is barely visible to the eye.

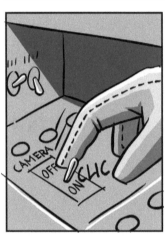

During the overflight, which can last up to nine hours, the ground crew is always strangely silent. The relief is when the pilot returns unharmed.

There he is!

The pilot is usually physically and emotionally exhausted.

LATER, WHEN POWERS RETURNS FROM ANOTHER OVERFLIGHT ...

A message for you, Powers.

What?

Powers can arrange for them to meet at least every other weekend in Athens.

1957 shows an increase in U-2 activity. There are new bases in Lahore and Peshawar, Pakistan.

The U-2 is now additionally equipped with an ejection seat. Black paint to avoid light reflection should make it more difficult to identify in the sky.

In their spare time, the pilots go on excursions to the countless Roman ruins, go duck hunting, fishing or swimming and snorkeling in the nearby Mediterranean Sea.

But the area is not without its dangers. Once, some of the pilots go fishing and are attacked overnight by Kurds who take everything away from them. (even the blankets).

ATHENS, SPRING 1957

Hello Frank, Already here?

Yes, I am. I caught an earlier bus at the airport.

I was going to call you yesterday, but I couldn't reach you.

Oh, I ... was busy.

37

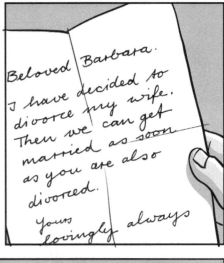

In August 1957, Barbara and Frank fly to America for a short vacation.

On August 26, 1957, the Soviet Union announces the successful launch of an intercontinental ballistic missile.

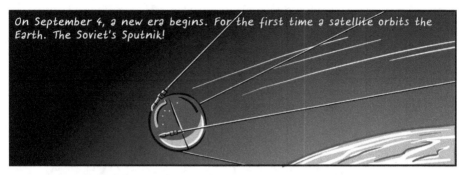

On September 4, a new era begins. For the first time a satellite orbits the Earth. The Soviet's Sputnik!

Barely a month later, Sputnik 2 carries the first living payload in orbit around the Earth: the dog Laika.

With these events, the U-2 gains renewed importance. The U.S. government awards the pilots the "Distinguished Flying Cross," a coveted award for special service.

BACK AT THE AIR BASE IN INCIRLIK

In "Soviet Aviation," the journal of the Soviet Air Force, a report was printed about the U-2.

It is called the "Black Lady of Espionage."

40

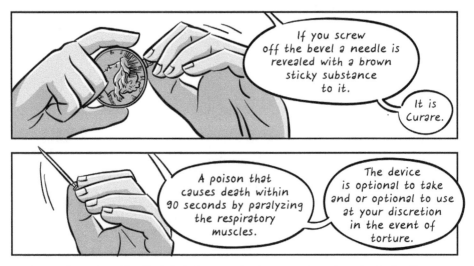

In September 1958, the Soviet Union conducts several nuclear tests in the Arctic. The U.S. pilots are transferred for three weeks to Bodø in Norway and collect measurement data and atomic samples with the U-2.

In November 1958, the pilots extend their contracts for another year. The number of U-2 missions declines.

Starting in 1959, the new U-2s are equipped with a more powerful engine with the aim of compensating for the weight of the many technical devices.

42

The pilot started a test flight from Atsugi* and wanted to attempt to set a new altitude record.

It succeeded, but the fuel was not enough to return to the base, and he had to land on a glider airfield.

And then?

Of course, the landing became public, and the Japanese press wondered why a weather research aircraft had no identification on it.

Flights are becoming fewer and fewer. The pilots extend their contracts for another year.

NOVEMBER 1959

I have made the following flight changes to pass on to you.

In the future there will always be two pilots that prepare for a flight at the same time. Should the pilot be unable to fly because of health reasons, the second will take his place.

I have a question.

Please.

What if something goes wrong and one of us goes down inside the Soviet Union?

* U-2 base in Japan.

44

In survival training, the pilots are prepared for possible scenarios: Equipped only with parachutes and emergency rations, they are dropped in two groups in a Turkish wasteland.

Power's group copes better with the situation. When food rations run low they replenish their supplies in a sugar beet field. After a while they find shelter in a village and are invited to dinner by the locals. They reach their destination on rented donkeys.

The other group is less fortunate. Some locals claim they saw them jump from airplanes and call the Turkish police, who arrest them as Soviet spies.

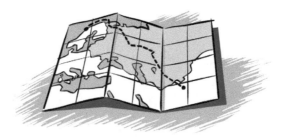

Peshawar-Bodø

In late April 1960, in the run-up to the Paris "peace summit" with U.S. President Eisenhower and Soviet Premier Khrushchev, the U.S. plans, after a long pause, for two U-2 reconnaissance flights over Soviet territory. Bob Ericson and Francis Gary Powers are scheduled as pilots. Ericson pilots the first mission, which, apart from visual contact with Soviet fighter planes, goes off without a hitch.

The second mission involves more risks: Powers' flight path leads from Peshawar in Pakistan to Bodø in Norway, overflying the entire width of the Soviet Union for the first time. The CIA thinks this is a vital flight path so that President Eisenhower can be better prepared for the upcoming Paris Summit talks.

TUESDAY, APRIL 27, 1960, MORNING.

Shaving kit, warm clothes. $100 should be enough.

Are you going to our news director's going-away party?

It isn't until May 1. I should be back here by then.

So, until then, take care.

You too, so long.

The twenty-member team flies to Peshawar on a C-130 turboprop.

VRRRRRRRR

U.S. AIR FORCE

WEDNESDAY, APRIL 28, 4 P.M.
The flight is scheduled for the next morning at 6 a.m.

Ericson and I are going to go to sleep. Wake us up at 2:00 a.m.

It's 2 a.m.

Weather is bad.

We have to postpone the flight till tomorrow.

THURSDAY 4 P.M.

Wake us again at 2 a.m.

All clear.

FRIDAY AFTER 2 A.M.

The flight is again postponed.

FRIDAY AFTERNOON

The flight will not take place on Saturday. Does anyone want to play poker?

Sure.

I'll call.

I'm out.

Hey, Bob, was everything normal when you flew my old lady here?

I had to get a spare plane, Article #360.

The one that crash landed at the glider airfield in Japan?

The one that always has new quirks? The one that does not use all its fuel?

Saturday, Powers and Ericson go to bed early again.

MAY 1, EARLY MORNING

This will be my only meal. It is 9 hours to Norway.

The doctor considers Powers to be in optimal shape.

Due to changing wind directions the navigation of the U-2 is adjusted.

Bob Ericson, the backup pilot, will acknowledge Power's radio click.

Everything is running normally.

If there are fuel tank problems ...

... you can shorten the route and fly directly over Sweden and Finland to Norway.

This will save a few minutes. You can land anywhere except in the Soviet Union.

Do you want the silver dollar?

I've never taken it, but ...

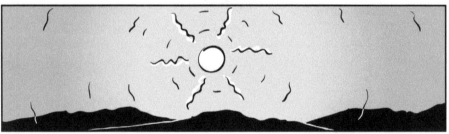

54

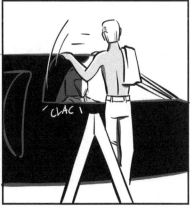

AT 70,500 FEET* ALTITUDE

Finally some cooler air.

Powers turns on the autopilot and completes the flight log. It's May 1, 1960.
* (21,450 meters)

The U-2 is equipped with a kind of periscope, through which the area under the airplane can be observed.

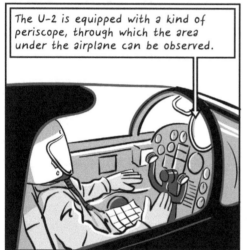

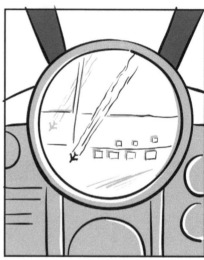

The cloud cover closes again for another two and a half hours. About 50 miles* south of Chelyabinsk the clouds disappear.

* (80 kilometers)

...the autopilot fails and the nose of the airplane lifts.

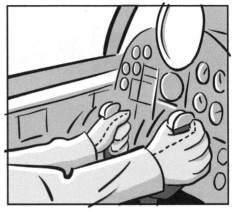

Powers corrects manually and turns the autopilot back on.

15 MINUTES LATER

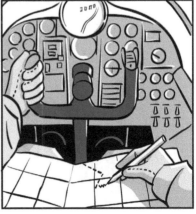

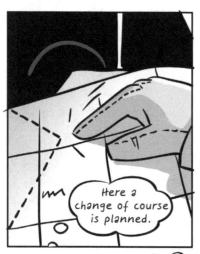

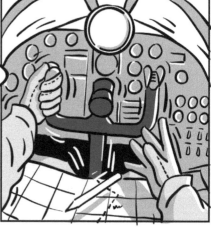

65

I will not use the ejection seat. I will climb out.

34000 Feet*.

Now the self-destruct button.

70 seconds are short; better loosen the seat belt first.

O29

Power's vision is massively impaired; his helmet visor is frozen over.

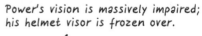

* (10,360 meters)

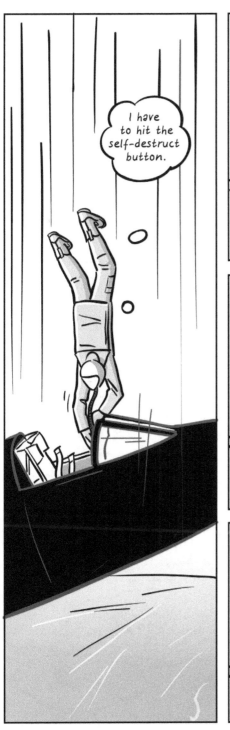

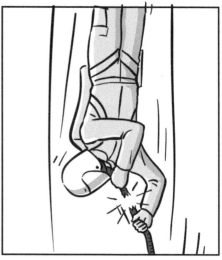

* (4,500 meters)

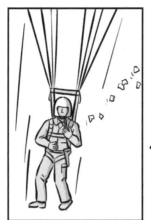

About two hours later, Powers is taken to Sverdlovsk. There he is searched once more, and the needle is found and placed in a file envelope. An English-speaking gentleman appears.

In captivity

The initial questioning is finally ended by a telephone call. Powers is taken to Moscow to Lubyanka prison (in the headquarters of the KGB secret police).

Again, he is stripped and thoroughly searched. He receives a worn, somewhat too big suit. Then he is led into an interrogation room.

* (20,700 meters) Powers is lying in order not to endanger possible later flights (the maximum flight altitude is close to 75,000 feet (22,860 meters)).

After about three hours, the interrogation takes an unexpected turn.

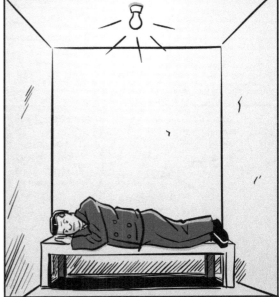

Powers is awakened by the opening of the cell door. A little old lady enters and brings a pot of tea with sugar and later a slice of bread and a boiled egg. Powers, however, has no appetite. After additional questioning, he is given a tour of the city, accompanied by an interpreter, a driver and two guards.

The following days, Powers is interrogated by different people with the same questions over and over again.

On May 5, Soviet Premier Nikita Khrushchev announces:

We have shot down an American spy plane over Soviet territory.*

The American authorities assume the plane was destroyed by the shootdown and Powers was killed.
They claim that the plane was collecting weather data.
On May 7, the Soviet Union presents the living pilot and the spy equipment from the plane wreckage.

Nikita Khrushchev demands an apology from U.S. President Dwight D. Eisenhower. When this fails to materialize, he storms out of the Paris Summit meeting between representatives of the USA, USSR, United Kingdom, and France.

Barbara has returned to the USA in the meantime.

Jesus, what will they do with him?

They will torture him, put him on trial and condemn him to death!

* An SA-2 missile comes close enough to damage the U-2 tail section.

Parts of the wrecked plane and Power's equipment are displayed at Gorky Park in an exhibition.

On August 17, 1960, Francis Gary Powers' 31st birthday, a large show trial begins. His wife Barbara, her mother, and his parents arrive from the USA to attend the trial.

Because of his sincere confession of guilt and genuine remorse, Francis Gary Powers escapes execution.

The sentence is: three years in prison and seven years hard labor.

Ten years!

August 24 brings a surprise. Powers is offered to see his wife again before she returns to the USA. He is taken to another prison in Moscow.

Early in the morning of September 9. Powers will be transported to Vladimir Central Prison located 150 miles* east of Moscow. There he is assigned a cellmate named Zigurd Krumnish, who speaks not only English and Russian, but also Latvian, German, French, Esperanto, and some Spanish. Zigurd was living in Latvia when in 1941 the Germans occupied Latvia. Most Latvians spoke fluent German and believed they were being liberated. In 1944 the Soviets reconquered Latvia, whereupon Zigurd joined the German army and fought against the Soviets. After the end of the war he became a guard soldier on a British base. Finally he was taken by boat to Latvia to help bring down down the Soviet regime. After one-and-a-half years in hiding he was caught by the Soviets and interrogated for three years.

Powers makes a deal with Zigurd that he would teach him Russian and Powers would help him to improve his English. Together, they share the 8 foot by 12 foot** cell number 31.

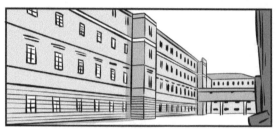

* (241 kilometers) ** (2.5 meters by 3.5 meters)

Vladimir Central Prison 9.23.1960

Dearest Barbara, how happy I am
You ... ...
no... ...
Ma...

II

one as the other. At 6 o'clock in the
morning Radio Moscow sounds from
the loudspeakers. As soon as we are
dressed, we are escorted to the first
trip to the toilet. Between 7:30 and
8 a.m. breakfast: soup or porridge.
At 10 a.m. we are allowed to go out for
two hours in a 15-foot by 20-foot courtyard.*
Lunch usually consists of soup and
a plate of cabbage, noodles, rice or
mashed potatoes, and some milk. Once
a week there is a small piece of meat.
The afternoons are quite slowly. For dinner
there are potatoes or cabbage. After that
comes the second trip to the toilet.
Every ten days we get fresh underwear
and socks. Once a week we are checked
by a doctor and once a month the
American embassy sends me a care
package with magazines, books, writing
materials, cigarettes, toothpaste, and soap.

*(4.5 meters by 6 meters)

A KGB colonel comes every two weeks.

*Powers makes a total of three rugs during his imprisonment.

JANUARY 22.

Here in *Pravda* a portion of Kennedy's speech is printed. It couldn't be better for you. Khrushchev even met with US Ambassador Thompson. This is a good omen.

JANUARY 23.

Look at this. So many Christmas cards!*

I think there is chewing gum in there.

What is gum?

I'll show you.

PLOPP

PFFFFFF

Ha, ha. Doesn't seem so easy.

JANUARY 27.

The two American USAF pilots who were shot down by the Soviets on July 1, 1960 were released.

And me?

MARCH 31.

After a two-month hiatus, Powers finally receives another letter from Barbara.

Why does she always keep me waiting?

* A columnist in America had called for Francis Gary Powers not to be forgotten at Christmas.

APRIL 18. Khrushchev's voice rang out on Radio Moscow.

«ВУЕРА АМЕРИКАНСАЯ АРМИЯ ПОПЫТАЛАСЬ ВТОРГНУТСЯ НА КУБУ»*

He said, yesterday American troops launched an invasion of Cuba at the Bay of Pigs.

This destroys all my hopes for a release.

JULY 1. not find out ~~~~ ~~~~
discussed at the K.K. meeting
June 3. But I had a call from
.... the attorney in N.Y. He is
in touch with .... in East Germany
and .... is working for a
release from there and Mr. Donovan
.... this end. He told me he
will soon receive a letter from
.... in East Germany.

Love Always Your Pa

P.S.: I have left out some names
that I do not want to mention in
this letter. We will do our best to
help you.

August 1961: Start of construction of the Berlin Wall.

In October Powers receives a letter from Barbara's sister.

Dear Francis.
I regret to inform you that Barbara's
drinking has gotten out of control.
She had a fight with your mother.
Under these circumstances medical
treatment was the best thing for
her and we took her to the psychiat.
department of Augusta University
Hospital. I am sorry to tell you thi
but we saw no other solution.

Best regards

CHRISTMAS

Look, my mother has given you gloves for Christmas.

Mr. Powers

Oh!

*Translation P. 98

90

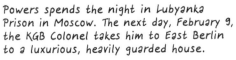

Powers spends the night in Lubyanka Prison in Moscow. The next day, February 9, the KGB Colonel takes him to East Berlin to a luxurious, heavily guarded house.

Glienicker Bridge

Welcome back to the West, Mr. Powers.

YOU AR
SECTO
ВЫ ОС
CEKT
AU
QUITTE
SIE VERL

My name is Donovan. I was Colonel Abel's attorney who you passed on the bridge.

I led the negotiations with the Soviets for this exchange.

I am glad to meet you.

Do my wife and my parents know about my release?

No, not yet.

94

Epilogue

In the USA, Powers is first questioned by the CIA and
USAF about the exact circumstances of the shootdown.
The suspicion that Powers disclosed more than his
oath of secrecy allowed is not true.

Powers talks with his wife Barbara, who has begun
drinking again, and they agree to divorce.

In 1963, he marries Claudia "Sue" Edwards, a former
psychologist for the CIA, and takes up a position as
a test pilot for Lockheed.

In 1970, he writes the book "Operation Overflight: A
Memoir of the U-2 Incident."

In 1976, he takes a job as a helicopter pilot at the
California television news station K-NBC.

In 1977, his helicopter runs out of gas, crashes,
killing him and the cameraman. Powers tried to
autorotate but in order to avoid children playing
baseball below, he deviated from the landing spot
losing any control being
provided through
autorotation. He is
survived by his wife,
his daughter "Claudia
Dee Powers" and his
son "Francis Gary
Powers, Jr." who
founded The Cold War
Museum (www.coldwar.
org) near Washington,
DC in 1996.

Mr. Powers,
how high were you
flying when you
were hit?

Not high
enough,
ha ha.

Translation of Russian texts

Page II: "Take care."

Page 70: "Were there two of you?" (In fact, by mistake, one of
their own MIG-19s was shot down).

Page 73: "Where is your plane?"
"Where are you from?"
"Are you hurt?"
"I'll take that."
"Can you bring us a glass of water, comrade?"
"Will do."

Page 74: "Cigarette?"
"Laika."
"Are you American?"

Page 76: "Undress, please."

Page 92: "Yesterday, American troops attempted an invasion of
Cuba."

Appendix:

Special features of the U-2.
Survival pack.
Glossary.

Special features of the U-2

Due to the extreme altitude at which U-2 pilots operate, a pressure suit made of stitch-resistant rubberized fabric is part of their basic equipment. This suit is intended to be worn in the event of a loss of pressure in the cockpit or in the event of an emergency ejection for survival. However, the pressure suit severely restricts the pilot's freedom of movement, so that he can only enter or leave the aircraft with the help of an assistant. To reduce the nitrogen content in his blood, the pilot must breathe pure oxygen for at least 90 minutes before each flight.

At the usual operational altitude of 70,000 – 75,000 feet, the low air density at that altitude places the U-2 aerodynamically in what is known in aviation circles as the "coffin corner." The slightest decrease in airspeed can lead to a loss of lift and places the aircraft in danger of descending into the range of hostile fighter jets and missiles. This is known as an engine flame out and the pilots can only restart the engine at lower altitudes if this happens. Vibrations that can tear apart the plane can also occur if the plane flies too fast. The pilot can control this only if

The cameras, ready for installation in the aircraft fuselage.

he knows the exact speed of his aircraft. The landing is very demanding, as it is carried out on two wheels mounted one behind the other.

The pilots affectionately refer to the U-2 as the "Dragon Lady." Flying it, they say, is sometimes like dancing with a lady and sometimes like fighting with a dragon.

* (approx. 21,300 to 22,900 meters)

The survival pack*

The survival pack was located in the seat
and contained:
- A collapsible life raft
- Clothing
- Water and food for a limited time
- Compass
- Signal fires
- Matches in waterproof containers
- Chemicals for starting a fire with damp wood
- First aid kit with morphine, bandages
  and water purification tablets
- An American silk flag with the following
  message in 14 languages:
  I am an American and I do not speak your
  language.
  I need food, shelter, help.
  I pose no danger to you.
  I have no animosity toward your people.
  Your help will be rewarded.
- 7500 rubles
- 48 gold coins Francs Napoleon
- 4 gold wrist watches and finger rings as
  objects of exchange
- one pistol caliber 22 with silencer and
  holster
- a survival knife (hunting knife)

Lighter, cigarettes, pocket knife and the wristwatch
in the picture belonged to Powers.

* The Survival Pack is on display at the Border Guard Museum in Moscow.

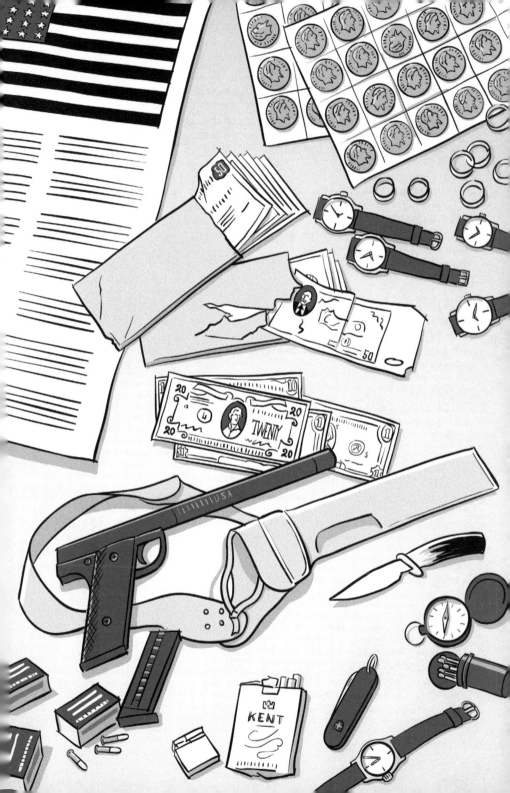

Glossary

Area 51:
In the southern Nevada desert which was kept secret by the government for a long time. The US Air Force tested its latest experimental aircraft there.

CIA:
U.S. Central Intelligence Agency.

Khrushchev:
Nikita Sergeyevich Khrushchev was the Premier of the Soviet Union 1958 to 1964.

GDR:
German Democratic Republic. Created four years after World War II ended. Overseen by the Soviets. Located in the Soviet occupation zone.

Eisenhower:
Dwight D. Eisenhower was President of the United States of America 1953 to 1961.

Glienicker Bridge:
Connection across the Havel River between Berlin and Potsdam. Separated East and West during the Cold War.

Kennedy:
John F. Kennedy, President of the United States of America 1961 until his assassination in 1963.

Cuba:
In 1959, Cuban guerrillas led by Fidel Castro, overthrew Cuban dictator Fulgencio Batista. Castro then became the new Dictator of Cuba.

As a result, the U.S. refused Castro a requested loan and supported the Cuban opposition, which led to the Bay of Pigs invasion in April 1961 that ended in a fiasco.

In response to a 1960 U.S. imposed ban on exporting oil to Cuba and a total ban on imports, the Soviet Union promised Castro economic and military assistance for Cuba.

In October 1962, U-2 aircraft were deployed over Cuba and provided proof that the Soviets had begun to establish missile bases. This resulted in the Cuban Missile Crisis, which almost led to a nuclear war.

Lovelace Clinic:
Clinic where U-2 pilots and later U.S. astronauts from NASA were put through strict physical and psychological tests.

Pravda:
Translates as "Truth;" was the official Soviet state run newspaper from 1912 to 1991 of the Central Committee of the Communist Party and the largest newspaper of the Soviet Union.

Commemorative plaque at the Glienicker Bridge.

BERLINER GEDENKTAFEL

Die von 1904 bis 1907 errichtete

GLIENICKER BRÜCKE

wurde im Zweiten Weltkrieg zerstört
und 1949 als „Brücke der Einheit" wieder eröffnet.
Die Machthaber der DDR, die ihr diesen Namen gaben
verhinderten jahrzehntelang die Einheit Deutschlands.
Nach dem Mauerbau 1961 durfte die Brücke nur noch
von alliierten Militärs und Diplomaten passiert werden.
Durch die friedliche Revolution in der DDR
ist die „Glienicker Brücke"
seit dem 10. November 1989 wieder für jedermann offen.

Text On the Commemorative Plaque

BERLIN COMMEMORATIVE PLAQUE

The bridge built from 1904 to 1907
GLIENICKER BRIDGE
was destroyed in World War II
and reopened in 1949 as the "Bridge of Unity."
The rulers of the GDR who gave it this name
prevented the unification of Germany for decades.
After the construction of the Berlin Wall in 1961,
the bridge could only be used by
allied military personnel and diplomats.
Due to the peaceful revolution in the GDR
the "Glienicker Bridge" has been
open to everyone again since November 10, 1989.

Bibliography, sources and further reading

"Spy Pilot: Francis Gary Powers, the U-2 Incident, and a Controversial Cold War Legacy" by Francis Gary Powers, Jr and Keith Dunnavant (National Book Network, 2019).

"Letters from a Soviet Prison: The Personal Journal and Private Correspondence of CIA U-2 Pilot Francis Gary Powers" by Francis Gary Powers, Jr. and Doug Campbell (LULU, 2017).

"Operation Overflight" by Francis Gary Powers (Brassey's Ink. 2004).

"The Secret War" by Sanche de Gramont (G. P. Putnam's Sons Inc. 1962).

"Strangers On A Bridge, The Case Of Colonel Abel" by James B. Donovan (Atheneum House, Inc., 1964). AERO, Issue 147 (Marshall Cavendish International Ltd. 1986)

Internet

Francis Gary Powers Jr's Website: www.GaryPowers.com
Walter Pfenninger's Website: www.pfenninger-illu.ch
The Cold War Museum®: www.coldwar.org
The SAC and Aerospace Museum: www.sac.org
The International Spy Museum: www.spymuseum.org
Spy Pilot: www.spypilotbook.com

About the U-2:
www.lockheedmartin.com/en-us/products/u2-dragon-lady.html
Beale AFB: www.beale.af.mil
Chris Pocock: www.dragonladyhistory.com
Road Runners Association: www.roadrunnersinternationale.com/u-2/u-2_science_7.html
Wikipedia: https://en.wikipedia.org/wiki/Lockheed_U-2

About Area 51:
Road Runners International: www.roadrunnersinternationale.com/area51.html
Wikipedia: https://en.wikipedia.org/wiki/Area_51

Related Links:

About the Cuban Missile Crisis:
https://en.wikipedia.org/wiki/Cuban_Missile_Crisis

About the Glienicker Bridge:
https://en.wikipedia.org/wiki/Glienicke_Bridge

Details of Power's 1977 helicopter crash:
www.check-six.com/Crash_Sites/Powers-N4TV.htm

CIA: www.cia.gov

FSB (New KGB): wwwgovernment.ru/en/department/113/

About the Co-authors

Francis Gary Powers, Jr.

Born June 5, 1965, Gary is the author of Letters from a Soviet Prison (2017) and Spy Pilot (2019). Gary is the Founder and Chairman Emeritus of The Cold War Museum located at Vint Hill, VA. He is the Chairman of the Presidential Advisory Committee for the Cold War Theme Study which assists the National Park Service to identify historic Cold War sites for preservation. Gary is the past President and CEO of the Vienna Tysons Corner Regional Chamber of Commerce (2000-2005) and in 2015, he consulted for a Steven Spielberg thriller, Bridge of Spies, about the 1962 spy exchange between KGB spy Rudolph Abel and CIA U-2 pilot Francis Gary Powers, Sr. He holds a Bachelor's Degree in Philosophy and Master's Degrees in Public Administration and U.S. History. Gary lectures internationally, appears regularly on C-SPAN, the History and Discovery channels. He is married with one son.

Walter Pfenninger

Born April 8, 1964, on Lake Zurich, Switzerland. Painting and drawing has always been his passion. After his training as a graphic designer, he worked in various advertising agencies in and around Zurich. For more than 20 years he has worked as a freelance illustrator and graphic designer for magazines, advertising agencies and publishing houses. He found the story of Francis Gary Powers so incredibly exciting that he simply had to turn it into a graphic novel. In 2012, on the 50th anniversary of the exchange of agents on the Glienicker Bridge, he published the graphic novel „Feindgebiet" (the German edition of Enemy Territory) with Zwerchfell Verlag. Walter lives with his wife Monika in Zurich-Höngg.